Sacagawea
Meet an American Legend

Carin T. Ford

Enslow Publishers, Inc.

40 Industrial Road   PO Box 38
Box 398   Aldershot
Berkeley Heights, NJ 07922   Hants GU12 6BP
USA   UK

http://www.enslow.com

Library of Congress Cataloging-in-Publication Data

Ford, Carin T.
　　Sacagawea : meet an American legend / Carin T. Ford.
　　　　p. cm. — (Meeting famous people)
　　Summary: A biography of the Shoshoni woman who helped to guide the Lewis and Clark
Expedition through the Northwest Territory of the United States in the early nineteenth century.
　　ISBN 0-7660-2004-5 (hardcover)
　　1. Sacagawea, 1786–1884—Juvenile literature. 2. Lewis and Clark Expedition (1804–1806)—
Juvenile literature. 3. Shoshoni women—Biography—Juvenile literature. 4. Shoshoni Indians—
Biography—Juvenile literature. [1. Sacagawea, 1786–1884. 2. Shoshoni Indians—Biography.
3. Indians of North America—Biography. 4. Women—Biography. 5. Lewis and Clark Expedition
(1804–1806)]　　I. Title. II. Series.
　　F592.7.S123F67 2003
　　978.004'9745'0092—dc21
　　　　　　　[B]
　　　　　　　　　　　　　　　　　　　　　　　　　　　　　2002008395

Printed in the United States of America

10 9 8 7 6 5 4 3 2 1

To Our Readers: We have done our best to make sure all Internet Addresses in this book were active
and appropriate when we went to press. However, the author and the publisher have no control over
and assume no liability for the material available on those Internet sites or on other Web sites they may
link to. Any comments or suggestions can be sent by e-mail to comments@enslow.com or to the
address on the back cover.

Every effort has been made to locate all copyright holders of material used in this book. If any errors
or omissions have occurred, corrections will be made in future editions of this book.

Illustration Credits: American Philosophical Society, p. 16T; © 1999 Artville, LLC, pp. 11, 24; Charles
M. Russell, *Lewis and Clark Expedition.* From the collection of Gilcrease Museum, Tulsa, Okla.,
pp. 20–21; Charles M. Russell, *Lewis and Clark on the Lower Columbia,* 1905, watercolor, 1961.195,
Copyright © Amon Carter Museum, Fort Worth Tex., p. 14; Denver Public Library, Western History
Collection, call no. X-33784, p. 4; Drawing by George Henry in *Sacajawea,* by Harold P. Howard,
Published by the University of Oklahoma Press, Norman, Okla., 1971, pp. 3 (detail), 12; Golden Dollar
Obverse © 1999 United States Mint. All rights reserved. Used with permission, p. 27; Library of
Congress, pp. 6, 7, 10T, 10B, 18, 25, 26, 28; Montana Historical Society, Helena, Mont., p. 22; Oregon
State Archives, Highway Division Records, Photo #3295, pp. 16–17; State Historical Society of North
Dakota 85.22, p. 8.

Cover Credits: Denver Public Library, Western History Collection, call no. X-33784 (portrait)

Table of Contents

1 Captured!. 5

2 On the River 9

3 Hard Times 15

4 End of the Trail. 19

5 Journey Home. 23

Timeline. 29

Words to Know 30

Learn More About Sacagawea. 31
    (Books and Internet Addresses)

Index. 32

The name Sacagawea means Bird Woman.

Chapter 1

Captured!

O ne day, when Sacagawea was about twelve years old, she was out searching for food. Gathering food was an important job for the women of her tribe, the Shoshone Indians. Suddenly, enemies from another tribe began to attack. Sacagawea tried to run away, but she could not escape from the Hidatsa warriors.

Sacagawea was born in Idaho around 1788. As a

The Shoshone Indians lived in tepees. These tents were made of animal skins.

child, she learned about roots, seeds, grasses, insects, and berries that were safe to eat. Shoshone women also cooked, sewed, made baskets, and cared for the children.

The men of the tribe were hunters and fishermen. They killed fish and small animals for food. The Shoshones lived in tepees and moved to different places each season to find food.

The Hidatsa warriors kidnapped Sacagawea on a

prairie near Three Forks, Montana. Then they took her hundreds of miles away from her family. The Hidatsa village was near Bismarck, North Dakota. There, Sacagawea was adopted and lived as a member of the Hidatsa tribe.

This Hidatsa warrior is dressed for a ceremony called the Dog Dance.

The Hidatsas were farmers. They did not move from place to place to find food. Their homes were large, round lodges made of earth. The men were hunters, artists, and traders. The women grew corn, beans, squash, and other crops. They also made pottery and baskets.

Sacagawea lived with the Hidatsas for a few years. She learned their ways and their language. When she was about fifteen, she became the wife of a French Canadian man named

Toussaint Charbonneau (too-sont shar-bun-o). He was in his forties and was living with the Hidatsas as a fur trader. He already had one or two other wives.

Some stories say that Charbonneau bought Sacagawea from the Hidatsas. Others say that he was playing a gambling game with some Hidatsa men. He won the game—and his prize was getting Sacagawea as his wife.

With the Hidatsas, Sacagawea lived in a round, earth-covered lodge. A few families shared each home.

Chapter 2

On the River

Sacagawea was about sixteen when she and her husband met two American explorers. Their names were Meriwether Lewis and William Clark. The men had been asked by President Thomas Jefferson to explore the land west of the Mississippi River. This large area was called the Louisiana Territory. The president asked Lewis and Clark to find a route from St. Louis, Missouri, to the Pacific Ocean.

Meriwether Lewis, above, and William Clark called their trip the Journey of Discovery.

He wanted to know what the land was like.

The explorers and about forty other men had begun traveling up the Missouri River in May 1804. By November, the river was beginning to freeze. They could not continue their trip until the ice on the river melted and broke up. They decided to build a fort and spend the winter in North Dakota. They called it Fort Mandan.

Charbonneau went to meet Lewis and Clark. He said he wanted to work for them. He could speak some Indian languages. He offered to help them talk to the Indians they would meet on their journey.

Lewis and Clark asked Sacagawea

to come along, too, because she knew the Shoshone language. Lewis and Clark wanted her to help them buy horses from the Shoshones. They would need horses to travel across the Rocky Mountains on their way to the Pacific Ocean.

Lewis and Clark were asked to explore and map the Louisiana Territory.

Not much has been recorded about Sacagawea's life. But Lewis and Clark kept journals of their trip, and that is how we know about her.

Sacagawea stayed at the fort during the winter. On February 11, 1805, she had a baby boy named Jean Baptiste. Clark nicknamed him "Pomp."

The ice on the river broke up after a few months. Sacagawea and the others began the journey west toward the Pacific Ocean. She was the only woman on the trip with Lewis and Clark.

The explorers traveled fifteen to twenty miles a day. They went by canoe and also walked along the shore.

Sacagawea carried her baby, Pomp, in a cradleboard on her back.

Sacagawea was very helpful. She dug into the ground with a stick and found roots to eat. She also found wild onions, berries, and plums for the explorers.

Sacagawea's name was hard to say, so Clark called her "Janey."

One day in May 1805, a storm suddenly came up. The winds and heavy rain knocked one of the canoes on its side. Many important supplies spilled into the river.

Charbonneau panicked. He was not a good swimmer. But Sacagawea, with the baby on her back, stayed calm. She grabbed many of the books, tools, and medicines that had fallen into the water. Lewis wrote in his journal that Sacagawea was very brave. Six days later, the explorers named part of the Musselshell River "the Sacagawea" in her honor. (It is now called Crooked Creek.)

Sacagawea helped Lewis and Clark by speaking to other Indians they met on their trip.

Chapter 3

Hard Times

Sacagawea and the exploring party continued to make their way up the Missouri River. They traveled through North Dakota into Montana. The journey was getting harder with each passing day.

Everyone was very tired. Many of the men were sick. Some had cuts, bruises, and sprains. Others came down with colds, fevers, stomachaches, and the flu.

Lewis also drew pictures in his journals.

Bugs were everywhere. Mosquitoes, flies, and fleas bit the travelers. And there were rattlesnakes and grizzly bears nearby.

In early June 1805, Sacagawea became very sick. Her stomach hurt, her fingers and arms shook, and she was weak. Lewis gave her water to drink. He also spread bark and some medicines on a cloth. Then he put the cloth on Sacagawea. By the end of June, Sacagawea was feeling well enough to go fishing.

The explorers now needed to carry the canoes around some waterfalls. It was hard work. They

made carts from the trees around them. Then they put the canoes onto the carts and pulled them.

A sudden storm blasted the travelers with rain and hail. The heavy rain caused a flood. Sacagawea and her baby were nearly swept away by the strong rushing water. Sacagawea held Pomp in her arms while Clark pushed her up

Sometimes the canoes had to be carried around waterfalls. Sacagawea, below right, and the men walked.

a hill to safety. He worried about Sacagawea. The storm had left her wet and cold. Clark did not want her to get sick again.

The explorers knew they could not cross the Rocky Mountains without Indians to guide them.

The exploring party marched on. Their one goal now was to find the Shoshone Indians. They had to buy horses if they were ever going to cross the mountains and reach the ocean.

Chapter 4

End of the Trail

The date was July 22, 1805, and Sacagawea remembered this place. She had been kidnapped from this spot on the Montana prairie several years earlier. She told the explorers that they were on the right trail. Soon, they would find the Shoshones.

Sacagawea had taught Clark a few Shoshone words. Now he asked her how to say "white man." But the Shoshones had never seen a white man. They had no word for it. "*Tab-ba-bone*," she told him. The word probably meant "stranger."

In August, the travelers finally met the Shoshones. When Sacagawea saw her people, she became very excited.

The head of the tribe was Chief Cameahwait. He invited Lewis and Clark to meet with him in a tepee. Then the explorers sent for Sacagawea to speak the Shoshone language.

Sacagawea stared at the chief. Suddenly she jumped up and raced over to him. Cameahwait was her brother! Sacagawea hugged him and cried. He

told her that most of her family had died. But she was so happy to see her brother. She gave him a small lump of sugar she had been saving.

The Shoshones had very little food, and they were starving. But they were kind to the explorers. By the end of August, the explorers had traded clothing and guns for nearly thirty horses. With several Indians to guide them through the mountains, they continued their journey. Sacagawea now rode on a horse.

On September 3, it began to snow. With little food, the men were growing thin and weak. Two weeks later, the travelers came upon the Nez Percé Indians.

When they finally met the Shoshones, Sacagawea hugged her childhood friend Jumping Fish.

They bought dogs from the Nez Percé and ate them.

The first week of November 1805, the travelers finally saw the Pacific Ocean. Sacagawea had journeyed more than 4,000 miles with the explorers. The men voted about where to spend the winter. Sacagawea voted too. A camp was set up in Oregon. The travelers would rest there for three and a half months. Then they would head home.

Traveling with Sacagawea (seated at right) helped show that the explorers had come in peace. "No woman ever accompanies a war party of Indians," Clark wrote.

Chapter 5

Journey Home

Winter was a time for catching up. Lewis and Clark drew maps and wrote about the trees, fish, and birds they had seen. Some men stitched moccasins. Others cleaned and repaired their guns.

In early January 1806, the explorers heard that a whale had washed up on the shore. Clark hoped they might get some whale fat—called blubber—to eat. He decided to take some men down to the shore.

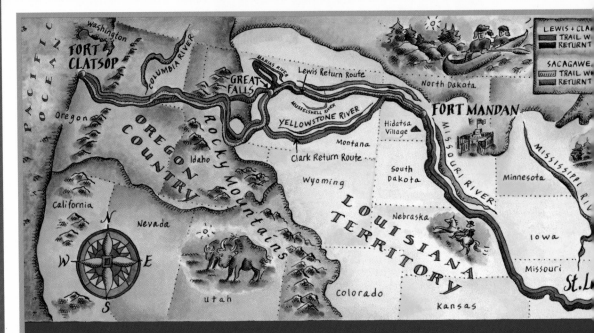

Sacagawea traveled thousands of miles with Lewis and Clark.

Sacagawea had asked for very little on this journey. Now she asked if she could go with the men to see the ocean and the whale. Clark agreed.

Mostly, life during the winter was dull. There was little food. Many of the men were sick.

Finally, in March, the travelers loaded their canoes for the trip home. On the way, Sacagawea's child became very sick. Pomp was fifteen months old and had a fever. His neck and throat were swollen. Lewis and Clark put onions, beeswax, and bear's oil on the boy's skin. By June, Pomp was feeling better.

Lewis dressed in Indian clothes for this painting.

Sacagawea and the explorers had to go back over the dangerous Rocky Mountains. This crossing was even harder than the last time. The snow was too deep, and there was no food. They had to turn back.

By summer, some Indian guides had been found to lead them across the Rockies. The trail took them out of the mountains into springs where hot water came out of the ground. Here, the explorers took their first hot baths in two years.

At this point, Lewis and Clark decided to split up. Lewis would take some men and go north to explore the Marias River area.

Sacagawea and her family stopped for a rest with the explorers at the mouth of the Columbia River.

Clark's group—which included Sacagawea—would go south along the Yellowstone River. The two parties would meet in North Dakota.

Sacagawea helped guide Clark and the others through Montana. She had once lived there and knew the area. Clark wrote that Sacagawea was of "great service to me as a pilot through this country."

The two exploring parties met again on August 12, 1806. They traveled together down the

Missouri River for the next few days. Soon, they reached Fort Mandan in North Dakota, where Sacagawea had begun her travels.

Lewis and Clark would now continue to make their way back to St. Louis, Missouri. President Jefferson had asked them to find a route from Missouri to the Pacific Ocean, and they had done it.

For Sacagawea, the journey was over. She had been gone for nearly two years.

Charbonneau, who had helped speak with the Indians and acted as cook, was paid $500. Sacagawea did not get anything. Clark wrote that Sacagawea deserved a "greater reward" for all she had done on the journey.

Clark did offer to take care of Sacagawea's son. He promised to send Pomp to school in St. Louis. Sacagawea

In 2000, the United States made this $1 coin to honor Sacagawea.

and Charbonneau agreed to send their son to Clark when he was a little older. And that is what they did.

But what happened to Sacagawea?

It is most likely that she died in South Dakota in 1812, at the age of twenty-five. She had recently given birth to a baby girl, Lizette.

This statue in City Park, Portland, Oregon, honors Sacagawea.

Some people say that Sacagawea went to live with the Shoshone Indians in Wyoming. There, she lived to be an old woman and died in 1884. Most historians today do not believe this story.

Sacagawea has become a much-loved figure in American history. She will always be remembered as a brave young woman who traveled with Lewis and Clark across the United States.

1788(?)~Sacagawea is born in Idaho.

1798(?)~Sacagawea is captured by the Hidatsa Indians.

1803~Thomas Jefferson buys the Louisiana Territory from France.

1804~Lewis and Clark begin their journey to find a route from St. Louis, Missouri, to the Pacific Ocean. Sacagawea joins the explorers in the fall.

1805~Sacagawea gives birth to a son, Jean Baptiste.

1806~Sacagawea helps guide Clark and other members of the exploring party through Montana.

1812~Sacagawea dies in South Dakota.

blubber—The thick layer of fat on whales.

Hidatsas—A group of Indians that was once part of the Crow tribe. They lived along the Upper Missouri River in North Dakota.

journal—A diary of a person's experiences.

Louisiana Territory—The part of the United States that lies between the Mississippi River and the Rocky Mountains. President Thomas Jefferson bought this land from France in 1803.

moccasin—A soft slipper made of leather.

Shoshones—A group of Indians, also known as the Snake Nation, who lived on both sides of the Rocky Mountains.

Learn More

Books

Adler, David A. *A Picture Book of Sacagawea.* New York: Holiday House, 2000.

Gleiter, Jan. *Sacagawea: First Biographies.* Austin, Texas: Raintree Steck-Vaughn, 1997.

Lourie, Peter. *On the Trail of Sacagawea.* Honesdale, Penn.: Boyds Mills Press, 2001.

Internet Addresses

The Life of Sacagawea
<http://www.usmint.gov/mint_programs/golden_dollar_coin/index.cfm?action=about_sacagawea>

Lewis and Clark
<http://www.pbs.org/lewisandclark/>

Index

B

Bismarck, North
  Dakota, 7

C

Cameahwait, Chief
  (brother), 20–21
Charbonneau, Jean
  Baptiste ("Pomp")
  (son), 12, 17,
  24–25, 27–28
Charbonneau, Lizette
  (daughter), 28
Charbonneau,
  Toussaint
  (husband), 7–8, 10,
  13, 27–28
Clark, William, 9–13,
  17–18, 19–20,
  23–24, 25–26,
  27–28

F

Fort Mandan, 10, 12,
  27

H

Hidatsa Indians, 5,
  6–8

J

Jefferson, Thomas,
  9–10, 27

L

Lewis, Meriwether,
  9–13, 16, 20, 23,
  25, 27, 28
Louisiana Territory,
  9, 11

M

maps, pp. 11, 24
Marias River, 25
Mississippi River, 9
Missouri River, 10,
  15, 27

N

Nez Percé Indians,
  21–22

P

Pacific Ocean, 9, 11,
  12, 22, 27

R

Rocky Mountains,
  11, 18, 25

S

Sacagawea
  birth, 5
  childhood, 5–7
  death, 28
  kidnapping, 5,
    6–7
  marriage, 7–8
  travels, 12–13,
    15–18, 19–22,
    24–27
St. Louis, Missouri,
  9, 27
Shoshone Indians, 5,
  6, 11, 18, 19–21, 28

T

Three Forks,
  Montana, 7

Y

Yellowstone River,
  26